is item must be returned or red on or before the latest date shown

Francis Frith's

Around
Liverpool
& Merseyside

Photographic Memories

Francis Frith's

Around
Liverpool
& Merseyside

Cliff Hayes

First published in the United Kingdom in 2001 by
Frith Book Company Ltd

Hardback Edition 2001
ISBN 1-85937-351-8

Paperback Edition 2001
ISBN 1-85937-234-1

Reprinted in Paperback 2002, 2003, 2004

British Library Cataloguing in Publication Data

Francis Frith's Liverpool & Merseyside
Cliff Hayes

Frith Book Company Ltd
Frith's Barn, Teffont,
Salisbury, Wiltshire SP3 5QP
Tel: +44 (0) 1722 716 376
Email: info@francisfrith.co.uk
www.francisfrith.co.uk

Printed and bound in Great Britain

Front Cover: **LIVERPOOL**, *St George's Plateau c1881* 14071

*The colour-tinting is for illustrative purposes only, and is not intended
to be historically accurate*

AS WITH ANY HISTORICAL DATABASE THE FRITH ARCHIVE IS
CONSTANTLY BEING CORRECTED AND IMPROVED AND THE
PUBLISHERS WOULD WELCOME INFORMATION ON OMISSIONS
OR INACCURACIES

Contents

Francis Frith: Victorian Pioneer 7

Frith's Archive - A Unique Legacy 10

Liverpool & Merseyside 12

Buildings of Liverpool 13

Shipping & Ships 38

South & East of the City 43

North of the City 45

Over the Water 50

The Ship Canal 75

Halton, Widnes & Runcorn 78

Index 87

Free Mounted Print Voucher 91

Francis Frith: *Victorian Pioneer*

FRANCIS FRITH, Victorian founder of the world-famous photographic archive, was a complex and multi-talented man. A devout Quaker and a highly successful Victorian businessman, he was both philosophical by nature and pioneering in outlook.

By 1855 Francis Frith had already established a wholesale grocery business in Liverpool, and sold it for the astonishing sum of £200,000, which is the equivalent today of over £15,000,000. Now a very rich man, he was able to indulge his passion for travel. As a child he had pored over travel books written by early explorers, and his fancy and imagination had been stirred by family holidays to the sublime mountain regions of Wales and Scotland. 'What lands of spirit-stirring and enriching scenes and places!' he had written. He was to return to these scenes of grandeur in later years to 'recapture the thousands of vivid and tender memories', but with a different purpose. Now in his thirties, and captivated by the new science of photography, Frith set out on a series of pioneering journeys to the Nile regions that occupied him from 1856 until 1860.

Intrigue and Adventure

He took with him on his travels a specially-designed wicker carriage that acted as both dark-room and sleeping chamber. These far-flung journeys were packed with intrigue and adventure. In his life story, written when he was sixty-three, Frith tells of being held captive by bandits, and of fighting 'an awful midnight battle to the very point of surrender with a deadly pack of hungry, wild dogs'. Sporting flowing Arab costume, Frith arrived at Akaba by camel sixty years before Lawrence, where he encountered 'desert princes and rival sheikhs, blazing with jewel-hilted swords'.

During these extraordinary adventures he was assiduously exploring the desert regions bordering the Nile and patiently recording the antiquities and peoples with his camera. He was the first photographer to venture beyond the sixth cataract. Africa was still the mysterious 'Dark Continent', and Stanley and Livingstone's historic meeting was a decade into the future. The conditions for picture taking confound belief. He laboured for hours in his wicker dark-room in the sweltering heat of the desert, while the volatile chemicals fizzed dangerously in their trays. Often he was forced to work in remote tombs and caves where conditions were cooler. Back in London he exhibited his photographs and was 'rapturously cheered' by members of the Royal Society. His reputation as a photographer was made overnight. An eminent modern historian has likened their impact on the population of the time to that on our own generation of the first photographs taken on the surface of the moon.

Venture of a Life-Time

Characteristically, Frith quickly spotted the opportunity to create a new business as a specialist publisher of photographs. He lived in an era of immense and sometimes violent change. For the poor, in the early part of Victoria's reign, work was a drudge and the hours long, and people had precious little free time to enjoy themselves. Most had no transport other than a cart or gig at their disposal, and had not travelled far beyond the boundaries of their own town or village. However,

by the 1870s, the railways had threaded their way across the country, and Bank Holidays and half-day Saturdays had been made obligatory by Act of Parliament. All of a sudden the ordinary working man and his family were able to enjoy days out and see a little more of the world.

With characteristic business acumen, Francis Frith foresaw that these new tourists would enjoy having souvenirs to commemorate their days out. In 1860 he married Mary Ann Rosling and set out with the intention of photographing every city, town and village in Britain. For the next thirty years he travelled the country by train and by pony and trap, producing fine photographs of seaside resorts and beauty spots that were keenly bought by millions of Victorians. These prints were painstakingly pasted into family albums and pored over during the dark nights of winter, rekindling precious memories of summer excursions.

The Rise of Frith & Co

Frith's studio was soon supplying retail shops all over the country. To meet the demand he gathered about him a small team of photographers, and published the work of independent artist-photographers of the calibre of Roger Fenton and Francis Bedford. In order to gain some understanding of the scale of Frith's business one only has to look at the catalogue issued by Frith & Co in 1886: it runs to some 670 pages, listing not only many thousands of views of the British Isles but also many photographs of most European countries, and China, Japan, the USA and Canada – note the sample page shown above from the hand-written *Frith & Co* ledgers detailing pictures taken. By 1890 Frith had created the greatest specialist photographic publishing company in the world,

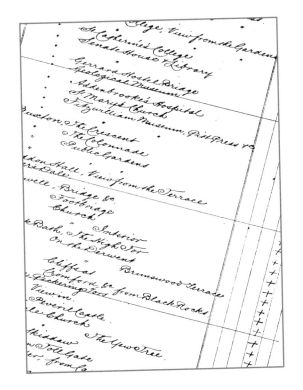

Frith's death, a new card measuring 5.5 x 3.5 inches became the standard format, but it was not until 1902 that the divided back came into being, with address and message on one face and a full-size illustration on the other. *Frith & Co* were in the vanguard of postcard development, and Frith's sons Eustace and Cyril continued their father's monumental task, expanding the number of views offered to the public and recording more and more places in Britain, as the coasts and countryside were opened up to mass travel.

Francis Frith died in 1898 at his villa in Cannes, his great project still growing. The archive he created continued in business for another seventy years. By 1970 it contained over a third of a million pictures of 7,000 cities, towns and villages. The massive photographic record Frith has left to us stands as a living monument to a special and very remarkable man.

with over 2,000 outlets – more than the combined number that Boots and W H Smith have today! The picture on the right shows the *Frith & Co* display board at Ingleton in the Yorkshire Dales (left of window). Beautifully constructed with a mahogany frame and gilt inserts, it could display up to a dozen local scenes.

Postcard Bonanza

The ever-popular holiday postcard we know today took many years to develop. In 1870 the Post Office issued the first plain cards, with a pre-printed stamp on one face. In 1894 they allowed other publishers' cards to be sent through the mail with an attached adhesive halfpenny stamp. Demand grew rapidly, and in 1895 a new size of postcard was permitted called the court card, but there was little room for illustration. In 1899, a year after

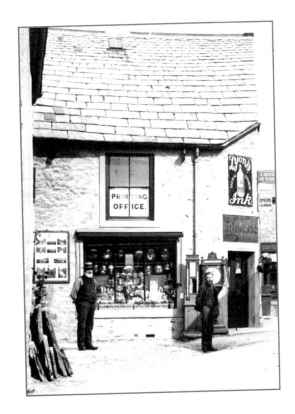

Frith's Archive: *A Unique Legacy*

FRANCIS FRITH'S legacy to us today is of immense significance and value, for the magnificent archive of evocative photographs he created provides a unique record of change in 7,000 cities, towns and villages throughout Britain over a century and more. Frith and his fellow studio photographers revisited locations many times down the years to update their views, compiling for us an enthralling and colourful pageant of British life and character.

We tend to think of Frith's sepia views of Britain as nostalgic, for most of us use them to conjure up memories of places in our own lives with which we have family associations. It often makes us forget that to Francis Frith they were records of daily life as it was actually being lived in the cities, towns and villages of his day. The Victorian age was one of great and often bewildering change for ordinary people, and though the pictures evoke an impression of slower times, life was as busy and hectic as it is today.

We are fortunate that Frith was a photographer of the people, dedicated to recording the minutiae of everyday life. For it is this sheer wealth of visual data, the painstaking chronicle of changes in dress, transport, street layouts, buildings, housing, engineering and landscape that captivates us so much today. His remarkable images offer us a powerful link with the past and with the lives of our ancestors.

Today's Technology

Computers have now made it possible for Frith's many thousands of images to be accessed almost instantly. In the Frith archive today, each photograph is carefully 'digitised' then stored on a CD Rom. Frith archivists can locate a single photograph amongst thousands within seconds. Views can be catalogued and sorted under a variety of categories of place and content to the immediate benefit of researchers.

Inexpensive reference prints can be created for them at the touch of a mouse button, and a wide range of books and other printed materials assembled and published for a wider, more general readership. The day-to-day workings of the archive are very different from how they were in Francis Frith's time: imagine the herculean task of sorting through eleven tons of glass negatives as Frith had to do to locate a particular sequence of pictures! Yet the archive still prides itself on maintaining the same high standards of excellence laid down by

See Frith at www.francisfrith.co.uk

Francis Frith, including the painstaking cataloguing and indexing of every view.

It is curious to reflect on how the internet now allows researchers in America and elsewhere greater instant access to the archive than Frith himself ever enjoyed. Many thousands of individual views can be called up on screen within seconds on one of the Frith internet sites, enabling people living continents away to revisit the streets of their ancestral home town, or view places in Britain where they have enjoyed holidays. Many overseas researchers welcome the chance to view special theme selections, such as transport, sports, costume and ancient monuments.

We are certain that Francis Frith would have heartily approved of these modern developments in imaging techniques, for he himself was always working at the very limits of Victorian photographic technology.

The Value of the Archive Today

Because of the benefits brought by the computer, Frith's images are increasingly studied by social historians, by researchers into genealogy and ancestory, by architects, town planners, and by teachers and schoolchildren involved in local history projects.

In addition, the archive offers every one of us an opportunity to examine the places where we and our families have lived and worked down the years. Highly successful in Frith's own era, the archive is now, a century and more on, entering a new phase of popularity.

The Past in Tune with the Future

Historians consider the Francis Frith Collection to be of prime national importance. It is the only archive of its kind remaining in private ownership and has been valued at a million pounds. However, this figure is now rapidly increasing as digital technology enables more and more people around the world to enjoy its benefits.

Francis Frith's archive is now housed in an historic timber barn in the beautiful village of Teffont in Wiltshire. Its founder would not recognize the archive office as it is today. In place of the many thousands of dusty boxes containing glass plate negatives and an all-pervading odour of photographic chemicals, there are now ranks of computer screens. He would be amazed to watch his images travelling round the world at unimaginable speeds through network and internet lines.

The archive's future is both bright and exciting. Francis Frith, with his unshakeable belief in making photographs available to the greatest number of people, would undoubtedly approve of what is being done today with his lifetime's work. His photographs, depicting our shared past, are now bringing pleasure and enlightenment to millions around the world a century and more after his death.

Liverpool & Merseyside
An Introduction

'Gateway to the British Empire', 'Second City in England', 'Door to the New World'. All these titles have been used to describe the city of Liverpool. Two hundred years ago it was a creek in the river; at the start of the 1900s Liverpool had built itself up into a world-class city with seven miles of docks full of ocean-going ships.

Liverpool was born thanks to a charter from King John in 1207. He promised land and equality to all who moved there, and thus the wonderful mix that makes up the people of Liverpool was started. It is a proud city, and an independent city; a city whose leading figures have upheld its proud traditions, and whose population included an unusually high number of philanthropists - together they forged a city of world-wide renown.

At the time of our first picture in this book, Liverpool would have had upwards of two hundred ships every week leaving for every corner of the great British Empire, and indeed the world. Ships went to Canada for corn, and carried iron goods to South America and Africa, and railway carriages to Brazil and South Africa. Ships loaded with generators and electrical goods for Australia and New Zealand brought wool and mutton back. India, China and Japan, Egypt - everywhere on the globe was covered by ships from Liverpool.

As the 19th century drew to a close, Liverpool was an exciting, vibrant city. Its citizens forged ahead with great building projects and modernisation. They electrified the Mersey Underground Railway, and they built an Overhead Railway to connect the ever-expanding dock area. Shipping companies built citadels that matched their world status. Insurance companies, whose fortunes waxed or waned with the fortunes of those shipping companies, vied with each other to build the grandest offices in the city centre.

Over the years, the great liners have gone, and the river front is quiet. Containerisation, mechanisation, in fact a whole new world is now taking over; but instead of going into a decline, Liverpool is once more thriving in a different way, and rising to new challenges that lie ahead. Liverpool today is one of the country's most successful and promising cities. It is a great place to be at the beginning of the 21st century.

Buildings of Liverpool

Liverpool
The Adelphi Hotel 1870 7841
This is the original Adelphi Hotel: it was built in c1840 on the site of Adelphi Gardens
by the Midland Railway Company, and was in direct competition with the London
North Western Railway Hotel, which was further along Lime Street. The hotel we see
here had a glass balcony, and a large portico entrance was added at the turn of the
century. This building was demolished in 1912. The present Adelphi Hotel was built
on the same site, with its architecture based on the style of an Atlantic liner.

Liverpool, The Synagogue c1874 7421

Liverpool
St George's Hall c1881 7813

Started in June 1838 to accommodate the Liverpool Music Festival, which was held every four years and had become a very popular event, St George's Hall is one of the greatest buildings in England. The designer Harvey Longsdale Elmes was only 23 when he won the design competition, firstly for the Music Hall and then for new Law Courts for Liverpool; he put the two buildings into one. Because of the change of plans and uses of the hall, the building was not started in earnest until 1842. Elmes never saw his magnificent work completed. The extra work put such a burden on him that he fell ill, and was sent on a sea journey to the West Indies to rest. He died just after arriving in Jamaica, and is laid to rest there. His work was taken over by C R Cockerell and the hall was opened on 18 September 1854. It is a strange mixture - concert hall, law courts, theatre, cells and jail - but it worked well, and is a marvellous and unique building.

**Liverpool
St George's Plateau
1881** 14071
It was planned that
around St George's Hall
there would be unbuilt
areas so as to show off
the Hall, the grandest of
the civic buildings. At
the back is St John's
Gardens, and in front is
the open area of St
George's Plateau. At the
time of our photograph,
it contained the
equestrian statues of
Prince Albert (1866)
and Queen Victoria
(1870), and the four
lions (1860) designed
by the man who put the
finishing touches to the
hall, Charles Robert
Cockerell. This was a
busy and important
area of Liverpool for a
century before our
photograph. The
cenotaph and the
reminder of two world
wars are still to come.

**Liverpool
The London & North
Western Railway
Hotel 1890** 26662
This view of St George's
Plateau shows the
London & North
Western Railway Hotel;
it was built by the
London & North
Western Railway
Company, and opened
in 1871. It was
designed by Liverpool-
born Alfred
Waterhouse. The
corporation thought
that this area was so
important that they paid
towards the cost of the
Storeton stone from the
Wirral for this French
Renaissance-style
building. It has three
hundred and thirty
rooms. After standing
empty for many years,
today the building is
owned by the John
Moores University, and
is used as student
accommodation.

Liverpool
The Exchange 1887 20001

We see here the open area outside the Liverpool Exchange, which
was known as Exchange Flags. It was a busy area thronged with
those whose business was the buying and selling of commodities.
Admiral Lord Horatio Nelson was a hero to the merchants of
Liverpool. His victories meant that they could ply their trade
throughout the world with complete freedom. When he died
fighting the French at Trafalgar in 1805, Liverpool sprang into
action and erected a monument to him: that bronze monument is
seen on the right of this picture. The inscription on it reads
'England expects every man to do his duty'. The statues and reliefs
around it represent Nelson's four great victories: Cape St Vincent,
the Nile, Copenhagen and Trafalgar. The figures are not slaves, but
prisoners taken in those battles.

Liverpool, The Custom House 1887 20015
Built in the late 1820s, the building we see here was Liverpool's fifth Customs & Excise collection building. Collecting tolls and excise duty was an important business, which demanded an important building. The Mersey Docks & Harbour Company also had their offices in the building at the time of our photograph. This was one of the buildings destroyed in the blitz of the Second World War, and had to be cleared away. Where this lovely building once stood is now an open space called Canning Place.

Liverpool, Dale Street 1887 20002
Dale Street is one of Liverpool's original seven streets, and is captured here full of hustle and bustle. The Municipal Building, with its tower and clock face, stands out further up the street. Built between 1860 and 1866, this building housed the financial offices of the corporation when the town hall proved to be too small for the ever-expanding city council. The 'Dale' that gave the street its name was at the far end by St John's Gardens.

Liverpool, Bold Street 1887 20010

Bold Street was for many years an elegant and elite shopping area. Here, taste and refinement were more important than price. We can also see St Luke's Church at the top of the street. This church was designed in 1802 by John Foster Senior. It was built by his son John after a lot of trouble in raising sufficient money - this extended the building period. This part of Bold Street once contained a Concert Hall, and in the 1960s the very best coffee bars were here. The street was named after the Bold family, who owned the land when the street was first laid out in the early 1700s.

Liverpool, The Sessions House 1887 19995

The Sessions House on William Brown Street is pictured here just three years after it opened. Designed by F & G Holme, its original purpose has now been forgotten. It was the home of the Lancashire Quarter Sessions, and has always been the poor relation of the buildings around it. It is an imposing classical-style building; the frontage has five bays, with a portico of four paired Corinthian columns, and the coat of arms of the Lancashire County Council over the entrance. It was for a time the Museum of Labour History. Today, the future of this ill-used building seems uncertain.

Liverpool
The Walker Art Gallery 1895   36647

The statues of Raphael and Michelangelo stand on the entrance steps to
the Walker Art Gallery in William Brown Street. Opened in 1877 to the
design of H H Vale, it was built as a single-storey Grecian-style building.
The bas-relief friezes along the front of the building represent four royal
visits to Liverpool. From right to left, beginning in Mill Lane, they show the
embarkation of King William III and his army at Hoylake in 1690;
continuing in William Brown Street are King John granting the first Charter
to the burgesses of Liverpool in 1207, the visit of Queen Victoria in 1851,
and the laying of the foundation stone of the Walker Art Gallery by the
Duke of Edinburgh in September 1874. On the roof over the main
entrance to the Gallery is an allegorical statue of Liverpool, by John
Warrington Wood. The large female figure in Carrara marble is seated on a
bale of cotton, crowned with a laurel wreath and holding a trident in one
hand, and a ship's propeller in the other. By her side is a bronze liver bird.

Liverpool, The William Brown Library and Museum 1895 36649

The William Brown Library, with its fine portico of six Corinthian columns, was built in 1860 to house the natural history collection of the 13th Earl of Derby; this had been bequeathed to the town in 1851. William Brown was a wealthy merchant who offered to pay for much of the cost of this grand enterprise, and he was rewarded for his generosity with the street and library named after him. There was much celebrating, and a day's holiday for the townspeople, when the building opened; it was the first of a magnificent row of public buildings in this street. It was badly bombed in 1941 and was rebuilt behind the original Grecian frontage.

Liverpool, The Picton Library and Reading Room 1895 36648

This building was named after Sir James Allanson Picton, antiquary and architect, knighted in 1881, the first chairman of the Liverpool Libraries Committee. He had devoted himself to the foundation of a free public library and museum for the people of Liverpool. The architect of this lovely round building was Cornelius Sherlock, and it was built between 1875 and 1879. Liverpool people nick-named it 'the gasometer', and the name stuck for many years. The building was provided by Sir William Brown, and the Corporation later added the Picton Reading Room in 1879.

Liverpool
The Pro-Cathedral 1890 26665
St Peter's was the name of this church, which gave Church Street its
name. Built in 1704, St Peter's was a very popular church and well
attended. In 1699, Liverpool was granted parish status; plans were made
to build a new church for this parish, which had broken away from
Walton. St Nicholas' Church was already there, but it was looked upon as
a seamen's church, a church for the merchants, so St Peter's was built for
the citizens. The money was raised by pre-selling the pews and boxes
inside to the better-off families of Liverpool. Before the church opened, a
small pew in a gallery cost an average of £33; at the end of the century it
fetched £110. The four doorways leading into the church were all in
different styles. After Liverpool became a city, this church was used as a
cathedral while a new grander building was planned. This building was
pulled down in the early 1920s.

Liverpool
Lime Street 1890

26661

St. George's Hall dominates the left side of our photograph, and the London North Western Hotel the right side. St George's Hall is unique, being a combination of two law courts, a concert hall, a theatre, a jail and cells. This is one of the finest buildings in the whole of Great Britain. Liverpool Council are doing a lot to make it more available to the public. The horse trams in the foreground would run for another decade before electric trams took their place. The Wellington column can be seen in the centre of the picture.

Liverpool
Church Street c1905

L60001

We are looking up Church Street from Lord Street, with the fascinating shop, Bunney's, on the left. Bunney's was the shop for unusual gifts and imported goods from all over the world, which came to Britain via Liverpool Docks. Bunney's specialised in oriental goods and 'novelties'; it was always an exciting shop to visit. The tall building further up the street on the left with its unusual sloped top is the Crompton Hotel, now the site of Marks & Spencers. This cross-roads was nick-named 'Holy Corner': (Our) Lord Street, Church Street, (White) Chapel and Paradise Street met here.

Liverpool
The Town Hall 1895 36650

The junction of Castle Street and Water Street, outside the Town Hall, has always been one of the busiest in Liverpool, and a natural meeting place. The balcony within the portico has seen some of the city's most memorable moments. Liverpool Football Club and Bill Shankley (and Everton as well in the 1930s) have waved to the crowds from here. The Beatles stood there in the late 1960s on their last combined visit to Liverpool - there was a crowd of a hundred thousand in Castle Street. The great names of Liverpool's history (Bessie Braddock, Lord Derby, Johnnie Walker, King Edward VII, Brian Epstein) have all acknowledged the cheers of the crowd from here. I believe that the figure on the top is Minerva, goddess of the sea and keeper of wisdom, although some say she is Britannia.

Liverpool
The Waterloo Column 1895 36645

The Waterloo Column, Liverpool's version of Nelson's Column in London, dominates this photograph. On it stands Arthur Wellesley, 1st Duke of Wellington, British general, statesman and Prime Minister. He is commemorated here as the victorious leader of the British forces in the Peninsular War 1808-14, which was caused by Napoleon's invasion of Portugal and Spain. The war finally ended in 1814 with Napoleon's abdication. Wellington's final victory against Napoleon was at Waterloo in 1815. The column stands 132ft high, and the Duke's statue is a further 15ft. It is said that the statue was forged using the metal from cannon captured at the battle of Waterloo. To the right of the column in the background is Commutation Row, which was built and named to celebrate the repeal of the window tax. Sad to say, it is now all cleared away for a modern building.

**Liverpool
Dale Street 1895**

36653

Dale Street was one of
the ancient streets of
the city and the main
road to all points south.
It contained many
fashionable and
important buildings, and
was the home of many
of the rising insurance
companies who did
business on the back of
the Liverpool shipping
companies. Royal
Insurance, Liverpool,
London & Globe, and
Prudential Insurance
were among those who
had their headquarters
here on this street. The
tower in the distance is
the Liverpool Municipal
Building, constructed
by the Corporation
when the Town Hall
proved too small.

**Liverpool
The Exchange 1895**

36655

This was known as Exchange Flags when it first opened at the end of the 1700s. The Exchange building seen here was the third on this site; it was designed by T H Wyatt, and put up in 1863. At one time you had to be invited to walk on the Exchange Flags. Much of the shipping and insurance business of the port was done on this square behind the Town Hall. In the middle of the Flags stands Nelson's monument, erected to the great man in 1813. It was Liverpool's first public monument, and was designed by Matthew Cotes Wyatt. The monument has four grilles which provide air vents for what was a tobacco warehouse under it. Also under part of the Flags is the secret war-time bunker where the operations for the north Atlantic were master-minded.

◄ **Liverpool**
The Overhead Railway 1895 36658
Here we have a close-up view of the
Overhead Railway, which ran from north
to south in the city and yet did not hold
up traffic going down to the Pier Head. It
was the first elevated electric railway in
Europe, and the first railway in Britain to
have automatic signalling, and there
were many other 'firsts' for this private
venture. It was initially opposed by the
city council, and by the Docks &
Harbour Board, both of whom it served
well for almost a century. You can see
the large ornate wooden Pier Head
Station on right of the photograph. The
very distinctive square Tower Building
was once the town house of the Stanley
family and Lord Derby.

Liverpool
The Floating Road 1895 36660

Our photographer is standing on the Prince's Landing Stage, looking up the floating road towards St Nicholas' Place and the church of Our Lady and St Nicholas at the top. We can also see the distinctive square Tower Building to the right. The floating road was supported on pontoons that rose and fell with the tide, which is high in our photo. This meant that wagons and lorries could drive straight onto the landing stage and board the luggage ferries for the journey over the Mersey, whatever the state of the tide. Can you make out the overhead railway, which had opened only two years earlier, running just below the church and tower building?

Liverpool, The Royal Liver Building c1955 L60019 ▲

The second of the Pier Head buildings was the Royal Liver Building. This must be one of the most recognisable buildings in Great Britain. Started in 1908, it was one of the world's first multi-storied buildings using re-enforced concrete for its construction. It was finished three years later in 1911. It was designed by Aubrey Thomas in a very free style, with the two mythical liver birds perched on the top of its towers. The liver birds are made of hammered copper plates bolted together, and are 18ft high. Their wingspan is 12ft across. They were made by a man named George Cowper, who was backed by the Bromsgrove Guild; once they were satisfied with their work, they dismantled the statues and rebuilt them on top of the Liver Building, fixing them into place with a rolled steel armature and 25ft of girders.

Liverpool
Entrance to the Mersey Tunnel c1955 L60002

We are looking straight into the Mersey Tunnel main entrance. Known as the Queensway Tunnel, it was at the time the only road tunnel under the River Mersey; it had opened in 1934. It soon replaced the car ferries and luggage boats. The tower of the Municipal Buildings on Dale Street dominates the sky-line to the left. At the time of our photograph, it cost 1s 6d for a car to go through the tunnel. It was a tanner (6d) for a motor bike and 9d for a motor bike and sidecar.

Shipping
& Ships

Liverpool, George's Dock c1881 14149
We see George's Dock from Mann Island. We can
just see St Nicholas' Church and the Tower Building
at the very far end. George's Dock was built out
from the original shore-line and opened in 1771.
At the time it was Liverpool's largest dock covering
26,793 square yards; it could hold, as we can see,
a considerable amount of shipping. The dock was
closed in 1900, and was filled in to give us George's
Parade (the Pier Head and the three large and
famous waterfront buildings that we have today).

Liverpool
HMS 'Hercules' 1890 24422
The Royal Navy once had much stronger ties with Liverpool than it does now. Quite often the whole of the Channel Fleet would exercise in the Irish Sea, and then have a three- or four-day visit to Liverpool. This would show the merchants and people of Liverpool that England had the power and might to look after its Merchant Fleet. Here the Frith photographer has captured two Royal Navy ships during one of those visits. HMS 'Hercules' was an apt name for an iron-clad battleship. Launched in 1868, she was twenty-two years old when our photograph was taken, and had been overtaken by newer ships with more and better guns that could cover the front and rear of the vessel. 'Hercules' could really only fire broadside.

Liverpool
HMS 'Bellisle' 1890 24421
We see HMS 'Bellisle' riding at anchor like a 'floating metal fortress' in the River Mersey as part of that same Royal Navy visit. With ten guns on board, she was heavier-armed than the 'Hercules', but she could only manage a top speed of eight knots even in good conditions. The fleet arrived in the Mersey on 27 September 1890 and left on 1 October 1890. Vice Admiral Sir Michael C Seymour and Rear Admiral Loftus Jones were in command.

Liverpool
SS 'Paris' The Smoking Room 1890 25088
Companies vied with each other for trade; some went for sheer elegance, and others offered cheap passages. The Inman Line had built its reputation on good solid safety and every home comfort. Started in 1850 by William Inman, of Liverpool, the company was sold to an American concern in 1886, so at the time of our photograph the Liverpool firm was being controlled from the other side of the Atlantic. Here we see the smoking room, the 'gentleman only' part of the accommodation for the 540 first-class passengers, or maybe the 200 second-class passengers - I doubt if the 1,000 steerage (cheap) passengers saw this room.

Liverpool, SS 'Adriatic' 1890 24417
The White Star Line started in Liverpool when Thomas Henry Ismay bought a bankrupt shipping company in 1868. He put money, new ships and new life into the company, and brought in the right partners and associates to found the successful business. White Star, whose motto was 'Ready and Steadfast', always aimed at the best. The SS 'Adriatic', built in 1872, was the fifth of their liners. We see her here just after she had had Second Class accommodation fitted. Not a lucky ship, she collided with Cunard's 'Parthia' at New York in October 1875, and in December the same year she hit the sailing ship 'Harvest Queen', drowning all on board. Her speed and metal bows got her into trouble again in July 1885, when she sank the brigantine 'G A Pink' - five crew died. Laid up at Birkenhead in 1890, she was taken to Preston for breaking up in 1899.

◄ **Liverpool
SS 'Paris' The Library
1890** 25087
The 'Paris' was a three-funnelled passenger liner. It was one of the first twin-screw ships to grace the north Atlantic run. The 10,798 gross ton liner had been in service for just two years when our photograph was taken.

The Ferry Boat to Egremont 1912 64443

The Egremont ferry started in 1835 from a small pier, and was taken over by Wallasey Corporation in 1862. A more substantial pier was built in 1876, which was replaced in 1909 just before our photograph was taken. The early corporation ferries were paddle-steamers, as is this one here. As there were two separate corporations running their parts of the ferry system, you could tell the corporation the boats belonged to by the funnel colours. There were eight piers and ferry points on the Wirral side of the river at the time of our photograph, including the one at Egremont.

Liverpool, The Ferry Boats c1955 L60021

Three of the famous Liverpool ferry boats are leaving the landing stage. The leading two are Wallasey ferries, one probably heading for New Brighton and packed with day trippers for the once-popular resort. It was nothing for 4,000 plus to visit New Brighton on a warm summer day in the mid 1950s. When naming ships, Birkenhead Corporation stuck to local names from the Wirral: 'Thurstaston', 'Hinterton', 'Claughton', and 'Bidston' were all names in the fleet at the time. Wallasey Corporation favoured names of flowers: the snub-nosed 'Royal Iris' was among the 1955 fleet, and names from the past include 'Bluebell', 'Snowdrop', 'Pansy', 'Rose' and 'Thistle'. The last steam ferry sailed in 1963, and the New Brighton service finished in 1971. The Merseyside Passenger Transport Executive took over the running of the ferries in December 1969. The ferries are still very much part of the Liverpool scene, and are in good hands. Heritage cruises, ship canal cruises and themed nights help keep the ferries exciting, as well as just a way to get to work.

South & East of the City

Liverpool
Sefton Park Bridge 1887 20050

Prize money of 300 guineas was announced for a competition in 1866 to design and lay out an area for 'the delight and pleasure of the public'. A Frenchman, M Andre, a gardener, and Liverpool's Mr Lewis Hornblower, architect, won that competition, and set about transforming the 233 acres bought from the Earl of Sefton. The cost of the land was £251,177 for 375 acres, but some of that was set aside for housing. The park was named after the Earl of Sefton, and is Liverpool's largest park, and larger than any of London's parks. It is also the most natural, with streams, small waterfalls and a rustic cast iron bridge over a ravine, shown here. An enclosed deer park, a boating lake, a cricket ground, and a review ground were among its original features when it was opened by HRH Prince Arthur (the third son of Queen Victoria) on Monday, 20 May 1872. The Prince stayed in Liverpool at the Grange, Wavertree, the home of Liverpool MP Mr S R Graves. After declaring the park open, the Prince visited a bazaar held to raise money for the new Royal Southern Hospital; he later watched 'horse-leaping' on the Parade Ground.

Liverpool, Sefton Park 1895 36673

The cast iron rustic bridge, built in 1870, has always been a much-photographed spot. Sefton Park has always had much to delight its visitors, and when the Palm House opened in 1896 thousands came to see it, along with the other glories of the Park. There is the Peter Pan statue, a pirate ship on the lake, and 'Children's Corner', with elves hidden amongst the flowers, which has charmed thousands of young Merseysiders over the last century or so. The Palm House is undergoing a complete restoration, and Liverpool can be glad that this great Victorian treasure has been saved to give pleasure to future generations.

Knowsley Hall 1890 26668

Knowsley is the home of the Stanley family, and is one of the most imposing of the large houses around Liverpool. It is also unique in that it is still today the home of Lord Derby (the title of the Stanley family). Here we have a good view of the large house which has welcomed so many kings, queens and princes over the years. Some came to stay as they journeyed around the country, but many more came as friends, to relax, or to take in a few days shooting. The older part of the hall is on the right, and though much of the estate is now given over to the Safari Park, the Hall still retains much of its family touch.

North of the City

Formby
The Old Lifeboat House c1960 F106030
Lying north from Liverpool were continuous golden sandy beaches.
Seaforth, Bootle, Crosby, Brighton-le-Sands, Blundell Sands and
Formby were easier to reach along the firm sand during the wet winter
months. It was a coastline that was used to the fierce storms of the Irish
Sea, and there were many shipwrecks. There were also many tales of
bravery and of daring rescues. Here we see the old lifeboat house on
Formby Beach, looking isolated and abandoned, as it was at this time.
The tower was a lookout tower, and many a sailor has been grateful
after being rescued by the men who once manned this station. Much of
the beach and the sand dunes behind are now a nature reserve, and
quite a lot of it is the property of the National Trust.

Formby
The Post Office and the Village c1955 F106003
The main Post Office was on Brows Lane. The name Formby is said
to derive from Icelandic or Scandinavian, and to mean 'the village
of the old wise man'. There is the possibility that it is derived from a
personal name, 'Forni', which was popular in Old English and in
Ireland. Note the parking restrictions on this narrow road: no
waiting is permitted on odd dates on one side of the road, and on
even dates on the other.

Formby
Brows Lane c1965 F106033
This view is from the same spot as our last photograph, but roughly ten years later. The narrow road has gone, widened in the name of progress. Sad to say, the wonderful trees on the older picture have gone, replaced with new shops and a parking bay for the ever-growing army of motorists using their cars to pop to the shops. The Post Office is still there in this photograph, and so is the District Bank next door - two disappearing amenities that we once, more or less, took for granted.

◀ **Freshfield
The Post Office c1965**
F117018
It is the furthest away of these three shops (on the corner) which is the Post Office. The shop nearest the camera is the local chemist, and the one in the middle is a pet and garden shop, whose merchandise includes rustic bird tables and garden furniture.

◀ **Freshfield
Rye Ground Lane c1965**

F117001

Freshfield is mainly a residential area just north of Formby; since World War Two it has grown so much that it now seems to have merged with Formby completely. It nestles right next to the Woodvale Airstrip, and has seen some exciting times over the years when it was a busy RAF Camp. Our photographer visited Freshfield over twenty-five years ago and caught these next scenes. Here we see the Grapes Hotel. The young men by the bike outside seem to be in uniform, so they probably came from the airbase.

◀ **Freshfield
Victoria Buildings c1965**

F117002

There was an area near Southport called Church, and the area now called Freshfield was originally Church Mere. Here we see Victoria Buildings on the corner of the road to the sand dunes, known as Formby Hills, and to Mad Wharf beyond them. Note the signal box just after the end of the building, and the level crossing gates between the two cars in our photograph. That is the Liverpool/Southport electric line, which has stations at Freshfield and Formby.

Over the Water

Birkenhead
Hamilton Square & Town Hall 1967 B399041

The well-laid-out Hamilton Square in the centre of
Birkenhead is named after the town's founder, John
Laird, in honour of his Scottish mother. In 1845,
when the houses were being completed, the square
was their private garden, and as the people moved
in they got a key. Space was left for a town hall to
be built, but it was 1883 before the foundation
stone was laid. It opened in February 1887 at a cost
of £43,067. The Town Hall, which incorporates the
magistrates' court and the council offices, is built of
Scottish granite and Storeton stone. In July 1901 it
caught fire; the tower collapsed, but it was quickly
rebuilt. It caught fire again in November 1935, but
the 200ft clock tower was again rebuilt. The
monument in the square is the town's memorial to
Queen Victoria. The council bought the gardens and
opened them up to the people; they made plans for
the cross, modelled on those erected to honour
Queen Eleanor, when Victoria died.

Birkenhead, Charing Cross 1967 B399044
The junction off Grange Road and Whetstone Lane (to the right) is known as Charing Cross. Grange Road was one of the main shopping streets in Birkenhead, and was very popular. The street is now pedestrianised, and with St John's Pavement in its centre is still a popular shopping area. The ornate building on the right was built as the North & South Wales Bank. On the left is the Grange Hotel, a large and well-known pub. It was a Birkenhead Brewery Hotel, a local firm founded in 1865 with a plant in Cleveland Street. 'BB' (Birkenhead Brewer) Stout was one of their successful products; we can see it advertised to the left of the entrance.

Birkenhead, Arrowe Park 1967 B399048
Arrowe Park is quite a few miles from the centre of Birkenhead. The estate was bought by Birkenhead Corporation in 1927 from the Leverhulme (Port Sunlight) family. The house seen here was built in c1840 by the Shaw family, who first owned the estate. In July 1929 the 423 acre park was turned over to the Boy Scouts for the world's first Scout Jamboree. Over 30,000 boys from all over the world gathered here, and the Prince of Wales, the Duke of Connaught, and Lord Baden-Powell himself visited them. Arrowe Park Hospital and an 18-hole golf course have since been created inside the park.

Birkenhead
Hamilton Square 1967 B399039
Birkenhead, the largest town on the Wirral, was the dream of one
man, John Laird. In about 1824 he came to a small hamlet of a few
hundred people, started his ship-building firm, and set about
planning a town. Because it was all laid out at the same time,
Birkenhead was very neat and orderly. It did have areas of back-to-
back houses for the newly-imported workers, but there were never
the slums of the older towns and cities. Soon Birkenhead became
a town. It was granted a Charter of Incorporation in 1877, and
plans for further growth were hatched. Hamilton Square was always
going to be where the town hall would be built, but it took forty
years before it was completed.

◀ **Birkenhead Storeton Road 1954**
B399007
The Half Way House Hotel is on the corner of Storeton Road and Woodchurch Road out towards Prenton. A large, solid half-timbered hotel, it was popular for functions and gatherings among the local population. Prenton Park, the home of Tranmere Rovers, is not far away, so the pub would be busy on home match days. The arrangement of the traffic light poles looks rather unusual.

Birkenhead
Woodchurch Road 1954 B399002

Birkenhead is a surprisingly large and sprawling town, and has taken in its outlying villages to become suburbs. In 1927, under the Birkenhead Extension Act, to celebrate its 50 years the town took in more outlying areas, thus doubling its original size of 1872. Woodchurch was one of those areas taken in. Here we see the shopping area. Many old favourites on the row include Waterworths the greengrocers and Dewhursts the butchers.

Birkenhead
The Cross-roads 1954
B399006

This is the cross roads of Storeton Road (out towards Storeton where the famous quarries are) and Woodchurch Road. The Half Way Hotel on the right is still there today. Our photograph seems to have a good selection of transport on it, with cars, waggons and delivery lorries, scooters, motor bikes and cycles - and shanks's pony.

Birkenhead
The Docks c1965 B399036

Birkenhead Docks were started on 23 October 1844 when the foundation stone was laid. Before that, ships sheltered or tied up in Bidston Pool, which lay between Birkenhead and Seacombe. John Laird started his ship-building in Bidston Pool; he moved to the Mersey when the dock building began here. The Docks were once an independent company, but money troubles forced them to join the Mersey Docks & Harbour Board and to be controlled from Liverpool. The arrival of the railway in the 1840s made the need for deep water docks even more essential. It was the Great Western Railway which ran into Birkenhead and the docks; it was the London Midland, Scottish which ran into Liverpool.

▼ **Birkenhead, The Mersey Tunnel c1965** B399027

This is the Birkenhead entrance to the Queensway Tunnel. This was the first road tunnel under the River Mersey, and was opened by King George V and Queen Mary in July 1934. To create the large tunnel entrance and the lead-up area, many back-to-back houses had to be pulled down; the town's library also had to be demolished. But the biggest job was moving the gas mains and sewers. The town hall tower shows above the entrance. The houses and shops on the right were pulled down shortly after our photograph was taken.

Wallasey ▶

The Village 1895 W164008

This is a lovely rural photograph taken in the old village of Wallasey. Wallasey has developed slowly, and even today there are still some of the older buildings dotted around in what still is considered by the locals as the village. Wirral was colonised by the Norsemen long ago, and many names reflect those invaders who settled here. From Old Wallasey (meaning 'the low land where the Welsh live') you can see over the Wirral to the Dee and Wales and the Irish Sea beyond. Workmen posing for the camera and an older sister taking her younger family for a walk, including a baby in a bassinette, complete our photograph.

▲ **Wallasey**

May Cottage and the Nook 1898 W164012

The coalman pauses between his deliveries. Village life carried on much as it always had done, even though not many miles away the industrial revolution was in full swing. Vegetables would be grown mostly by the villagers themselves in their own back gardens; most would bake their own bread and cakes. Their lives went slowly on, in an undisturbed rustic idyll.

◄ **Wallasey**
The Church and the Tower
c1873 8468
St Hilary's is the old parish church of Wallasey. There are not many churches dedicated to this saint, and this church is also unique because of its two towers. There has been a church on this site for over a thousand years. Twice a fire has destroyed the buildings: the lone tower dates from a church built in around 1530 which caught fire in the 1850s. The tower was saved, and the new church, seen behind, was built slightly away from the old tower.

◀ **Liscard**
The Roundabout c1960
W164048
This roundabout has always
been a very busy spot. Here
see it from Wallasey Road
looking up what has always
been known as Liscard Villa
even though it is a road. Th
captures a time when every
shopped on his or her local
high street, and out-of-town
shopping was unheard of. C
photographer has his back
the ABC Carlton Cinema, w
stood at this junction.

◀ Wallasey, St Hilary's Church c1950 W164501

As we look at the church from Broadway, we get a closer view of how large it is. This is explained by a need to accommodate the hundreds of summer visitors who came to this area, and who needed to attend church on a Sunday. We can see clearly the two castellated towers: the older tower on the right of the picture dates from the 16th century, and is noted for its gargoyles.

◀ Old Wallasey
▼ Wallasey Village c1960

W164063

In 1910 the Borough of Wallasey was formed. This took in the UDCs of Egremont, New Brighton, Leasowe, Poulton, Moreton, Seacombe and Wallasey. To pull it together and administer so many individual areas was a very hard task, and it took a strong-minded council several years to get things running smoothly. Technically, there is a Wallasey in Wallasey and a Liskard in Wallasey, and this does lead to some confusion over older photographs. Also, the High Streets have the quaint name 'the Village', so we have a road named Liskard Village, Upton Village etc.

Egremont, The Landing Stage 1890 24427

This stage was built to replace an original from 1835; it lasted until 1909, when it was replaced. When a tanker hit the pier in May 1932, it took a year to repair it. There was no hurry, because the Seacombe pier could be used - the passengers would go the last mile by bus. In 1940, during war-time blackouts, the pier was hit again, very badly, by a ship ready to form a convoy to cross the North Atlantic. This time the pier was abandoned, and before the war was over it had disappeared completely.

Egremont, From the Sands 1895 36685

Playing on the sands seems to be an enjoyment forgotten today, but here these youngsters certainly seem to be enjoying themselves on Egremont beach. The area was never as commercial as its sister New Brighton, but it was still a popular holiday destination. The black-and-white timbered building on the left of the picture is Old Mother Redcap's Inn, steeped in history, with stories of shipwrecks, sailor's gold and smugglers. It was pulled down in the 1970s, but they say that there is gold buried somewhere round here, and Old Mother Redcap's ghost still haunts the area.

Egremont, The Promenade 1898 41017

If we look closely at our top photograph, we will see that the turrets and tower of the New Brighton Tower building are missing. Though it opened in 1898, the building was not completed until a year later. Our bottom photograph is from 1902, and though the tower building is complete it was not to last much longer. The name Egremont was given to a big house built by John Askew, who bought land here. He called the house Egremont to remind him of where he was born in the Lake District. He also had a hand in developing New Brighton.

Egremont, The Promenade 1902 48662

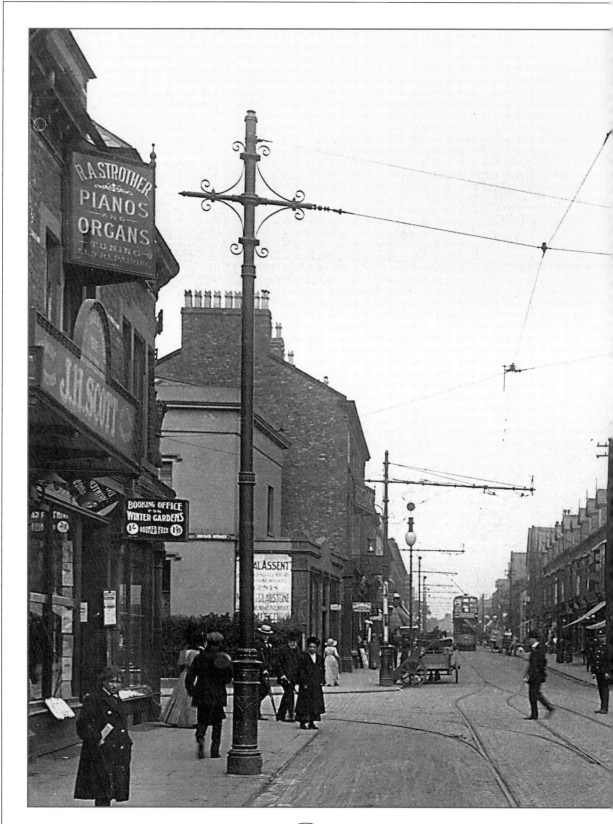

**Egremont
King Street 1912**
64429
Because Egremont was
a newly-laid-out town,
the streets were mostly
straight and wide. King
Street ran parallel to the
Promenade, and was a
very busy thoroughfare.
Here we see a Wallasey
tram on the crowded
single track part of the
street. Wallasey was
very proud of its
Corporation Transport
Department, and would
do anything to match or
better Birkenhead's
efforts. Though they are
now one, as Wirral,
there was for 75 years a
very healthy rivalry
between the two.

New Brighton, Victoria Road 1895 N14011
Like so much on this coast, New Brighton was developed from open waste space, and was laid out specifically to be an attraction. James Atherton was the man with the dream, helped and supported by John Askew. Though the original plans were very grand and exciting, money proved a problem. Costs kept on rising before income started to come in, and the large mansions planned became ordinary houses, and the exclusive hotels became boarding houses and cafes. Victoria Road led away from the pier; it was famous for its dozens of cafes, even into the 1950s.

New Brighton. The Fort 1886 14269
Also known as Perch Rock and the Battery, the Fort was, and still is, a very large landmark on the New Brighton shore. Completed in 1825 at a cost of £25,000, it was part of the defences on the River Mersey, and was used to store gunpowder for ships visiting Liverpool. It is a tribute to its designer and builder Captain John Kitson that it is so strong and solid today, 175 years later; it is now used as a museum.

New Brighton
The Beach 1887 20067
Having your photograph taken was part of a
holiday, and these booths would take your
photograph and turn out six or twelve copies in
about an hour. The beach was where the
unlicensed traders set up, and where the cheaper
end of the entertainments went on, including the
boxing booths and the travellers' fairground. To
many people, this was the only way to get family
photographs. The incoming tide, of course,
cleared the beach until the next low water.

New Brighton
The Lighthouse 1887 20069
Tradition says that a lighthouse was built on the sands here in the
early 1700s, but it collapsed into the sand. A ship carrying cotton
bales was shipwrecked off Wirral, and the bales washed ashore.
Wood and parts of the ship soon sank into the sand, but the bales
of cotton did not. Then grass started to grow on the cotton bales,
and this held firm in the sand. Bales of cotton were then
deliberately sunk into the foreshore, and a wall was built on them.
They did not sink, and the two lighthouses on this coast were built
on this same principle: Leasowe first, then New Brighton in 1827
at a cost of £27,000. We can see that the entrance is 40ft up the
lighthouse, and can only be reached by climbing an iron ladder
fixed to the outside of the 90ft structure.

New Brighton, The Pier and the Parade 1892 30416
The houses on the right were soon turned into cafes to serve the ever-growing numbers of holidaymakers. They would advertise breakfasts bigger than each other, vying with each other for customers. The row soon became known as 'the ham and egg parade', and very popular it was too. But as in all English seaside towns, package holidays abroad brought about the demise of these places. Eventually the row was bought by the council and pulled down to make way for the new promenade that they had planned.

New Brighton, General View 1892 30418
James Atherton, who bought the 170 acres of land on this north-east corner of Wirral, had to modify his original grand plans. He still ended up with a town built solely for entertainment, and for the newly-emerging holidaymakers. Egremont's James Askew put in more cash, but this could not stop the building of ordinary houses to rent or sell off and bring in much-needed revenue. It is thought that he named this new town to rival Brighton on the south coast, but his home in North Everton was next to Brighton le-Sands, a part of Liverpool, so maybe that is where the name came from.

**New Brighton
The Tower and the
Sands 1900** 45163
An Eiffel Tower at New
Brighton was part of the
original dream of James
Atherton as he planned
his new holiday resort.
It was started in 1896
and opened in 1898. At
631ft high, it was the
tallest structure in
Britain at the time.
Once again, money was
short, and maintenance
was haphazard. The
profits from the popular
tower and its athletic
track in the grounds
was used to prop up
other parts of the
scheme. During the
Great War (1914-18)
the tower was allowed
to rust and rot, and in
1918 it was declared
unsafe. No money
could be found to repair
the tower, and the local
council could not take it
on, or did not want to,
so in 1919 work started
on dismantling it. By
Easter 1921 it was
gone. The building
below the tower lasted
until a fire in April
1969.

◀ **New Brighton**
The Beach and the Pier c1960
N14024

There was something for everyone at New Brighton. On the beach there was a children's boating pool, and the Pier had a bar and an amusement palace on it. The Pier was built to accommodate the crowds, and was really two piers next to each other. The river at this point was prone to silting, and though no-one could know it at the time, this would prove to be a major problem. It was the main reason that the ferries gave up, at the end of Summer 1971. After this, the Pier soon fell into decay, and was later pulled down.

◄ New Brighton
The Front c1960 N14035

This is how I remember New Brighton. Arriving on the ferry, walking the promenade, we were teenagers trying to impress. It was cheap and tacky, but the arcades and fairground were just what we wanted. This side of the pier was the promenade, with the theatre, and the swimming baths. The other side, further up the Mersey, was the fairground and the large model railway, which carried children and their parents on what seemed a journey of miles, through jungle and adventure land.

▼ Port Sunlight
Post Office Corner c1960 P188066

Port Sunlight was the dream of William Lever, a man who believed that there was good in everyone; only the best would do for his workers and employees. He moved his soap-making factory from Warrington to Bromborough Dock around 1888, and then set about building homes for the workers. The estate covered 770 acres (including the works); when it was finished, it housed around 6,000 people. Every cottage was said to be different, and many different architects were employed to help turn a swampy muddy creek into a wonderful Garden Village. Here we see a few of those workers' houses and the post office.

◄ Port Sunlight
Christ Church c1960 P188053

William Lever, later Lord Leverhulme, added every amenity he could think of to the village. A club-house, library, hospital, youth club, gymnasium and swimming baths, all were included. The building Lord Leverhulme was said to be proudest of was Christ Church, the place of worship that he built for Port Sunlight. It looks much older than the century it was built in, and has a very solid yet charming feel to it. When Lady Lever died, William turned all his art treasures that he had collected over the years to the people and opened the Lady Lever Art Gallery. When he died in 1925, the porch that you can see to the left of the church became his resting place.

Eastham
Stanley Lane c1965 E9031

This is the old village centre. The unusual war memorial and cross are on the left, and the massively-buttressed tower of the parish church dominates the skyline. There was a church here in Norman times, and stones from that building were incorporated into this church. Its list of vicars goes back to 1316, and it records bishops back to the 7th century. The Eastham Gardens, down by the ferry, were very popular, and over the years attracted thousands of visitors. They lost some of their glamour at the start of the 20th century and became a bawdy place. When the visitor numbers declined, the ferry stopped running here and the pier was dismantled. The gardens closed soon after; today they are a country park.

◀ **Eastham**
The Church c1965 E9036

The Hooton branch of the Stanleys all lie here in the church, including Sir Rowland Stanley, who died aged 96 in 1613. It is inscribed on his brass grave plate that he saw his son's son's son settled in Hooton, and was the oldest Knight in all England. Among the gravestones are those of many young men who perished learning to fly at nearby Hooton Air Strip. Philip Thickness, the man who designed the Cunard building in Liverpool, also lies here. He designed the white stone crucifixion panel in the Stanley Chapel.

▼ **Irby**
The Old Post Office c1948 I42001

Most rationing had ended by now, but you still needed sweet coupons to spend your sixpence or shilling pocket money at this thatched Post Office and general stores. Irby is one of the many Scandinavian names on Wirral, and means 'place of the Irishmen', referring to Vikings who had previously lived in Ireland.

Upton, The Village c1955 U36002
Upton is an ancient Viking village just three miles from the Irish Sea. It had a windmill on the outskirts of the village, and an old gabled mansion which saw action for Cromwell's men during the siege of Chester. Birkenhead has spread out and almost overtaken the village today, but at the time of our photograph it still retained some of its independence.

Upton, The Village c1960 U36013
The Village, Upton is this quaintly-named road. It leads up to St Mary's, a 19th-century church with its handsome pulpit and a thousand-year-old runic Viking stone in a small showcase. T J Heseltine, the family butchers, is the shop on the left, and next to it is the well known firm of Melias, the confectioners. Rakes Lane goes off to the right. It is said to get its name from Rakes Hall, where gambling and drinking went on.

The Ship Canal

Eastham
The Dock c1965 E9504

As oil tankers got bigger and bigger in the early 1950s, some of them were difficult to handle on the Manchester Ship Canal. Eastham Oil Dock was constructed in 1954 to allow these larger tankers to discharge their cargoes without entering the Ship Canal. It was built on the landward side of the canal so that its pipes and equipment did not have to pass over or under the Manchester Ship Canal. As we can see in our photograph, the entrance is right next to the Ship Canal entrance lock. The top ship is in the Ship Canal lock, the other three are in Eastham Dock.

◀ **Ellesmere Port**
The Manchester Ship Canal c1955
E135033

The thirty-five mile long Manchester Ship Canal works as one great harbour, and ships moving up and down the canal have to register each movement with the control centre at Eastham. When it first opened, the Ship Canal gave countless industries on the Mersey a chance to import and export more easily and cheaply. Railway lines were laid along the dockside so that goods could be loaded and unloaded from boat to railway wagon. Ellesmere Port was a favourite dock for timber from Russia and Scandinavia; from here it was moved all over the north for house building. The railway lines may look rusty and abandoned, but the canal is still busy at this time.

◄ **Ellesmere Port**
Flour Mills
and the Docks c1955 E135009
Ellesmere Port was created when the Earl
of Ellesmere constructed a canal from
Ellesmere in Shropshire to meet the River
Mersey. It was constructed to bring the
goods from the potteries to Liverpool for
world-wide distribution. The small village
of Whitby, where the canal met the river,
was renamed Ellesmere Port. Here we
see the docks that linked the Ship Canal
with the Ellesmere Canal (now called the
Shropshire Union Canal), with the tall
flour mils in the background.

▲ **Ellesmere Port**
◄ **Dock Street c1955** E135022
The Ellesmere Canal was busy, and more and
more workers were needed to handle the
goods and repair the barges; thus the port
grew. Many of the Manchester Ship Canal
workers settled here, where there was plenty
of work to be had in the ever-spreading town.
Here we see Dock Street (it led down to the
old dock) looking slightly past its best. The
Ellesmere Port Motor Company premises are
on the left, but they look empty and deserted.
The town has a very pleasant civic centre and
shopping area, but today it has to compete
with the large Cheshire Oaks retail outlet
nearby. The docks are now a museum, and
well worth a visit.

Halton, Widnes & Runcorn

Widnes, West Bank 1923 73918
We are looking at West Bank and the Victoria
Promenade. This area had been regarded as a
holiday resort, and had been known as Wood-end
150 years before. The square tower, centre, is St
Mary's Church, built in 1908. A Mersey schooner is
heading for Spike Island and the St Helen's Canal
just behind it. Our photograph was taken from the
Transporter Bridge, which stood at the crossing
point for over fifty years. The building on the right
was the local cottage hospital for the very Welsh
community who lived in West Bank.

**Widnes
St Paul's Church
and the Free Library
1908** 59503
Victoria Square is in the
centre of Widnes. The
building on the left is
the library; the
Technical College is at
the side of it. The
church is St Paul's,
Widnes' parish church,
which opened in 1884
on land given in 1878
in the will of the late J G
Leigh. The building on
the far side of the
square is the Widnes &
Runcorn Co-operative
Society offices and
shops. The square, with
the town hall (out of
sight on the right), was
the centre of civic
occasions.

Runcorn, The Railway Bridge 1900 45433
The Widnes-Runcorn railway bridge is seen from the West Bank Docks, Widnes. The town of Runcorn is behind the bridge; the retaining wall of the Manchester Ship Canal can be seen along the edge of the River Mersey. The bridge was constructed from 1863-67; it opened on 21 May 1868, and was named the Ethelfleda Bridge, after a Celtic princess who ordered the very first ferry here. The three iron spans of this bridge (which is still in use today) weigh around 700 tons each, and the piers are sunk to a depth of 45ft into the solid rock of the river bed. The church spire is All Saints, Runcorn's parish church.

Runcorn, The Transporter Bridge c1906 43432A
The Transport Bridge Company was formed in 1899, and parliamentary approval was given in July 1900. Widnes Corporation gave £25,000 towards the scheme, and Runcorn gave £10,000. The transporter opened on 29 May 1905, but in 1911 the Widnes Runcorn Bridge Company transferred the transporter to Widnes Corporation; they strengthened it and added new electric motor. It was as the Widnes/Runcorn transporter when it re-opened on 21 May 1913. The ceremony was performed by Sir John Brunner, who had officiated at the original opening eight years previously. Widnes Corporation maintained and paid for the bridge until it closed in 1961. Here we see the bridge with its carrying platform near the Widnes side.

Runcorn
The Widnes/Runcorn Bridges c1960 R67043
Two of the three bridges which have spanned Runcorn Gap over
the River Mersey are seen from Runcorn. To the right is the
transporter bridge, which was dismantled in 1961 -2 months after
the new single-span road bridge opened on Saturday, 22 July 1961
by HRH Princess Alexandra. The road bridge had taken four years
to build, and was very much needed by the time it opened. Sunday
and holiday traffic heading to and from North Wales could take up
to two hours to cross. If only they had left the transporter standing;
it would have made a great attraction today, forty years later.

Runcorn, Weston Point c1955 R67019
We are looking from the Beacon Hill area. Down below, on what was once marsh land, and an area known as Duke's Fields, is not only the Manchester Ship Canal but the Waver Navigation Canal and the Runcorn Docks. Bridgewater House is to the right, and some of the ICI works to the left. The River Mersey has a large sweeping bend here. We can make out the Hale shoreline over on the far bank.

Runcorn, The Docks c1900 R67301
A real mixture of shipping make up this photograph of Weston Point Docks. The main waterway we see here is the Weaver Navigation, built so that the salt boats which floated down the River Weaver from Northwich and Nantwich could get back into those Cheshire towns without fighting the flow of the river. The lock in the foreground leads to the Manchester Ship Canal and the larger docks to the right. Guano and animal bones from South America were among the more unusual imports here, as well as the more usual cargoes of hides, soap, salt and leather.

Runcorn
Top Locks c1955 R67001

Top Locks was the end of the Bridgewater Canal system - it had come all the way from Manchester and Worsley. Top Locks was named thus because if its location at the top of a large set of locks which opened in about 1780; they brought boats from the River Mersey and Liverpool up to the Bridgewater Canal. In 1800, canal and river was the easiest way of travelling from Manchester to Liverpool in the winter. By the time of our photograph, the locks had been closed and filled in, so the canal finished here at Waterloo Bridge. The Waterloo Hotel is on the left on High Street. In 1961, the area's first Chinese restaurant opened in the small white buildings on the left. It cost half-a-crown for chicken chow mein with curry sauce.

Runcorn, Devonshire Place c1956 R67044
The top of the High Street was known officially as Devonshire Place, but the locals always called it Devonshire Square, even though it only had three sides. Our photographer is standing on Doctors Bridge over the Bridgewater Canal, and High Street runs left and right from the top of the square. Both the new high-level road bridge and the old transporter can be seen on our photograph. Today, Curiosities Bookshop can be found on the High Street to the right, opposite what was the La Scala Ballroom.

Halton, The Castle 1900 45439
Here we have a general view of Halton and its castle from the west. The castle was built by the new Norman lord of the manor of Halton, Nigel Fitzwilliam, in around 1071. The baronies of Halton and Widnes were combined in about 1200, and were later taken under the Duchy of Lancaster, where they remain today. The castle is owned by the Queen; there are plans to restore much of it and open it to the public. The views from up there are really breath-taking. The main castle gateway was used as a court and prison in 1274; the castle last saw action in 1643 in the Civil War. The Court House was restored and became the Castle Hotel. The large church on the right is St Mary's, erected in 1847.

Index

Adelphi Hotel 13

Birkenhead 50-51, 52, 53, 54-55, 56

Bold Street 22

Church Street 28-29

Custom House 21

Dale Street 21, 32-33

Eastham 72, 73, 75

Egremont 60, 61, 62-63

Ellesmere Port 76-77

Entrance to the Mersey Tunnel 37

Exchange 20, 34-35

Ferry Boats 42

Floating Road 36-37

Formby 45, 46, 47

Freshfield 48-49

George's Dock 38-39

Halton 86

HMS 'Bellisle' 40

HMS 'Hercules' 40

Irby 73

Knowsley Hall 44

Lime Street 26-27

Liscard 58

London & North Western Railway Hotel 18-19

New Brighton 64, 65, 66, 67, 68-69, 70-71

Overhead Railway 36

Picton Library & Reading Room 24

Port Sunlight 71

Pro-Cathedral 25

Royal Liver Building 37

Runcorn 82, 83, 84, 85, 86

Sefton Park 43, 44

Sessions House 22

SS 'Adriatic' 40

SS 'Paris' 40-41

St George's Hall 15

St George's Plateau 16-17

Synagogue 14

Town Hall 30

Upton 74

Walker Art Gallery 23

Wallasey 56-57, 58-59

Waterloo Column 31

Widnes 78-79, 80-81

William Brown Library & Museum 24

Frith Book Co Titles

www.francisfrith.co.uk

The Frith Book Company publishes over 100 new titles each year. A selection of those currently available is listed below. For latest catalogue please contact Frith Book Co.
Town Books 96 pages, approximately 100 photos. **County and Themed Books** 128 pages, approximately 150 photos (unless specified). All titles hardback with laminated case and jacket, except those indicated pb (paperback)

Title	ISBN	Price	Title	ISBN	Price
Amersham, Chesham & Rickmansworth (pb)	1-85937-340-2	£9.99	Devon (pb)	1-85937-297-x	£9.99
Andover (pb)	1-85937-292-9	£9.99	Devon Churches (pb)	1-85937-250-3	£9.99
Aylesbury (pb)	1-85937-227-9	£9.99	Dorchester (pb)	1-85937-307-0	£9.99
Barnstaple (pb)	1-85937-300-3	£9.99	Dorset (pb)	1-85937-269-4	£9.99
Basildon Living Memories (pb)	1-85937-515-4	£9.99	Dorset Coast (pb)	1-85937-299-6	£9.99
Bath (pb)	1-85937-419-0	£9.99	Dorset Living Memories (pb)	1-85937-584-7	£9.99
Bedford (pb)	1-85937-205-8	£9.99	Down the Severn (pb)	1-85937-560-x	£9.99
Bedfordshire Living Memories	1-85937-513-8	£14.99	Down The Thames (pb)	1-85937-278-3	£9.99
Belfast (pb)	1-85937-303-8	£9.99	Down the Trent	1-85937-311-9	£14.99
Berkshire (pb)	1-85937-191-4	£9.99	East Anglia (pb)	1-85937-265-1	£9.99
Berkshire Churches	1-85937-170-1	£17.99	East Grinstead (pb)	1-85937-138-8	£9.99
Berkshire Living Memories	1-85937-332-1	£14.99	East London	1-85937-080-2	£14.99
Black Country	1-85937-497-2	£12.99	East Sussex (pb)	1-85937-606-1	£9.99
Blackpool (pb)	1-85937-393-3	£9.99	Eastbourne (pb)	1-85937-399-2	£9.99
Bognor Regis (pb)	1-85937-431-x	£9.99	Edinburgh (pb)	1-85937-193-0	£8.99
Bournemouth (pb)	1-85937-545-6	£9.99	England In The 1880s	1-85937-331-3	£17.99
Bradford (pb)	1-85937-204-x	£9.99	Essex - Second Selection	1-85937-456-5	£14.99
Bridgend (pb)	1-85937-386-0	£7.99	Essex (pb)	1-85937-270-8	£9.99
Bridgwater (pb)	1-85937-305-4	£9.99	Essex Coast	1-85937-342-9	£14.99
Bridport (pb)	1-85937-327-5	£9.99	Essex Living Memories	1-85937-490-5	£14.99
Brighton (pb)	1-85937-192-2	£8.99	Exeter	1-85937-539-1	£9.99
Bristol (pb)	1-85937-264-3	£9.99	Exmoor (pb)	1-85937-608-8	£9.99
British Life A Century Ago (pb)	1-85937-213-9	£9.99	Falmouth (pb)	1-85937-594-4	£9.99
Buckinghamshire (pb)	1-85937-200-7	£9.99	Folkestone (pb)	1-85937-124-8	£9.99
Camberley (pb)	1-85937-222-8	£9.99	Frome (pb)	1-85937-317-8	£9.99
Cambridge (pb)	1-85937-422-0	£9.99	Glamorgan	1-85937-488-3	£14.99
Cambridgeshire (pb)	1-85937-420-4	£9.99	Glasgow (pb)	1-85937-190-6	£9.99
Cambridgeshire Villages	1-85937-523-5	£14.99	Glastonbury (pb)	1-85937-338-0	£7.99
Canals And Waterways (pb)	1-85937-291-0	£9.99	Gloucester (pb)	1-85937-232-5	£9.99
Canterbury Cathedral (pb)	1-85937-179-5	£9.99	Gloucestershire (pb)	1-85937-561-8	£9.99
Cardiff (pb)	1-85937-093-4	£9.99	Great Yarmouth (pb)	1-85937-426-3	£9.99
Carmarthenshire (pb)	1-85937-604-5	£9.99	Greater Manchester (pb)	1-85937-266-x	£9.99
Chelmsford (pb)	1-85937-310-0	£9.99	Guildford (pb)	1-85937-410-7	£9.99
Cheltenham (pb)	1-85937-095-0	£9.99	Hampshire (pb)	1-85937-279-1	£9.99
Cheshire (pb)	1-85937-271-6	£9.99	Harrogate (pb)	1-85937-423-9	£9.99
Chester (pb)	1-85937-382 8	£9.99	Hastings and Bexhill (pb)	1-85937-131-0	£9.99
Chesterfield (pb)	1-85937-378-x	£9.99	Heart of Lancashire (pb)	1-85937-197-3	£9.99
Chichester (pb)	1-85937-228-7	£9.99	Helston (pb)	1-85937-214-7	£9.99
Churches of East Cornwall (pb)	1-85937-249-x	£9.99	Hereford (pb)	1-85937-175-2	£9.99
Churches of Hampshire (pb)	1-85937-207-4	£9.99	Herefordshire (pb)	1-85937-567-7	£9.99
Cinque Ports & Two Ancient Towns	1-85937-492-1	£14.99	Herefordshire Living Memories	1-85937-514-6	£14.99
Colchester (pb)	1-85937-188-4	£8.99	Hertfordshire (pb)	1-85937-247-3	£9.99
Cornwall (pb)	1-85937-229-5	£9.99	Horsham (pb)	1-85937-432-8	£9.99
Cornwall Living Memories	1-85937-248-1	£14.99	Humberside (pb)	1-85937-605-3	£9.99
Cotswolds (pb)	1-85937-230-9	£9.99	Hythe, Romney Marsh, Ashford (pb)	1-85937-256-2	£9.99
Cotswolds Living Memories	1-85937-255-4	£14.99	Ipswich (pb)	1-85937-424-7	£9.99
County Durham (pb)	1-85937-398-4	£9.99	Isle of Man (pb)	1-85937-268-6	£9.99
Croydon Living Memories (pb)	1-85937-162-0	£9.99	Isle of Wight (pb)	1-85937-429-8	£9.99
Cumbria (pb)	1-85937-621-5	£9.99	Isle of Wight Living Memories	1-85937-304-6	£14.99
Derby (pb)	1-85937-367-4	£9.99	Kent (pb)	1-85937-189-2	£9.99
Derbyshire (pb)	1-85937-196-5	£9.99	Kent Living Memories(pb)	1-85937-401-8	£9.99
Derbyshire Living Memories	1-85937-330-5	£14.99	Kings Lynn (pb)	1-85937-334-8	£9.99

Available from your local bookshop or from the publisher

Frith Book Co Titles (continued)

Title	ISBN	Price
Lake District (pb)	1-85937-275-9	£9.99
Lancashire Living Memories	1-85937-335-6	£14.99
Lancaster, Morecambe, Heysham (pb)	1-85937-233-3	£9.99
Leeds (pb)	1-85937-202-3	£9.99
Leicester (pb)	1-85937-381-x	£9.99
Leicestershire & Rutland Living Memories	1-85937-500-6	£12.99
Leicestershire (pb)	1-85937-185-x	£9.99
Lighthouses	1-85937-257-0	£9.99
Lincoln (pb)	1-85937-380-1	£9.99
Lincolnshire (pb)	1-85937-433-6	£9.99
Liverpool and Merseyside (pb)	1-85937-234-1	£9.99
London (pb)	1-85937-183-3	£9.99
London Living Memories	1-85937-454-9	£14.99
Ludlow (pb)	1-85937-176-0	£9.99
Luton (pb)	1-85937-235-x	£9.99
Maidenhead (pb)	1-85937-339-9	£9.99
Maidstone (pb)	1-85937-391-7	£9.99
Manchester (pb)	1-85937-198-1	£9.99
Marlborough (pb)	1-85937-336-4	£9.99
Middlesex	1-85937-158-2	£14.99
Monmouthshire	1-85937-532-4	£14.99
New Forest (pb)	1-85937-390-9	£9.99
Newark (pb)	1-85937-366-6	£9.99
Newport, Wales (pb)	1-85937-258-9	£9.99
Newquay (pb)	1-85937-421-2	£9.99
Norfolk (pb)	1-85937-195-7	£9.99
Norfolk Broads	1-85937-486-7	£14.99
Norfolk Living Memories (pb)	1-85937-402-6	£9.99
North Buckinghamshire	1-85937-626-6	£14.99
North Devon Living Memories	1-85937-261-9	£14.99
North Hertfordshire	1-85937-547-2	£14.99
North London (pb)	1-85937-403-4	£9.99
North Somerset	1-85937-302-x	£14.99
North Wales (pb)	1-85937-298-8	£9.99
North Yorkshire (pb)	1-85937-236-8	£9.99
Northamptonshire Living Memories	1-85937-529-4	£14.99
Northamptonshire	1-85937-150-7	£14.99
Northumberland Tyne & Wear (pb)	1-85937-281-3	£9.99
Northumberland	1-85937-522-7	£14.99
Norwich (pb)	1-85937-194-9	£8.99
Nottingham (pb)	1-85937-324-0	£9.99
Nottinghamshire (pb)	1-85937-187-6	£9.99
Oxford (pb)	1-85937-411-5	£9.99
Oxfordshire (pb)	1-85937-430-1	£9.99
Oxfordshire Living Memories	1-85937-525-1	£14.99
Paignton (pb)	1-85937-374-7	£7.99
Peak District (pb)	1-85937-280-5	£9.99
Pembrokeshire	1-85937-262-7	£14.99
Penzance (pb)	1-85937-595-2	£9.99
Peterborough (pb)	1-85937-219-8	£9.99
Picturesque Harbours	1-85937-208-2	£14.99
Piers	1-85937-237-6	£17.99
Plymouth (pb)	1-85937-389-5	£9.99
Poole & Sandbanks (pb)	1-85937-251-1	£9.99
Preston (pb)	1-85937-212-0	£9.99
Reading (pb)	1-85937-238-4	£9.99
Redhill to Reigate (pb)	1-85937-596-0	£9.99
Ringwood (pb)	1-85937-384-4	£7.99
Romford (pb)	1-85937-319-4	£9.99
Royal Tunbridge Wells (pb)	1-85937-504-9	£9.99
Salisbury (pb)	1-85937-239-2	£9.99
Scarborough (pb)	1-85937-379-8	£9.99
Sevenoaks and Tonbridge (pb)	1-85937-392-5	£9.99
Sheffield & South Yorks (pb)	1-85937-267-8	£9.99
Sherborne (pb)	1-85937-301-1	£9.99
Shrewsbury (pb)	1-85937-325-9	£9.99
Shropshire (pb)	1-85937-326-7	£9.99
Shropshire Living Memories	1-85937-643-6	£14.99
Somerset	1-85937-153-1	£14.99
South Devon Coast	1-85937-107-8	£14.99
South Devon Living Memories (pb)	1-85937-609-6	£9.99
South East London (pb)	1-85937-263-5	£9.99
South Somerset	1-85937-318-6	£14.99
South Wales	1-85937-519-7	£14.99
Southampton (pb)	1-85937-427-1	£9.99
Southend (pb)	1-85937-313-5	£9.99
Southport (pb)	1-85937-425-5	£9.99
St Albans (pb)	1-85937-341-0	£9.99
St Ives (pb)	1-85937-415-8	£9.99
Stafford Living Memories (pb)	1-85937-503-0	£9.99
Staffordshire (pb)	1-85937-308-9	£9.99
Stourbridge (pb)	1-85937-530-8	£9.99
Stratford upon Avon (pb)	1-85937-388-7	£9.99
Suffolk (pb)	1-85937-221-x	£9.99
Suffolk Coast (pb)	1-85937-610-x	£9.99
Surrey (pb)	1-85937-240-6	£9.99
Surrey Living Memories	1-85937-328-3	£14.99
Sussex (pb)	1-85937-184-1	£9.99
Sutton (pb)	1-85937-337-2	£9.99
Swansea (pb)	1-85937-167-1	£9.99
Taunton (pb)	1-85937-314-3	£9.99
Tees Valley & Cleveland (pb)	1-85937-623-1	£9.99
Teignmouth (pb)	1-85937-370-4	£7.99
Thanet (pb)	1-85937-116-7	£9.99
Tiverton (pb)	1-85937-178-7	£9.99
Torbay (pb)	1-85937-597-9	£9.99
Truro (pb)	1-85937-598-7	£9.99
Victorian & Edwardian Dorset	1-85937-254-6	£14.99
Victorian & Edwardian Kent (pb)	1-85937-624-X	£9.99
Victorian & Edwardian Maritime Album (pb)	1-85937-622-3	£9.99
Victorian and Edwardian Sussex (pb)	1-85937-625-8	£9.99
Villages of Devon (pb)	1-85937-293-7	£9.99
Villages of Kent (pb)	1-85937-294-5	£9.99
Villages of Sussex (pb)	1-85937-295-3	£9.99
Warrington (pb)	1-85937-507-3	£9.99
Warwick (pb)	1-85937-518-9	£9.99
Warwickshire (pb)	1-85937-203-1	£9.99
Welsh Castles (pb)	1-85937-322-4	£9.99
West Midlands (pb)	1-85937-289-9	£9.99
West Sussex (pb)	1-85937-607-x	£9.99
West Yorkshire (pb)	1-85937-201-5	£9.99
Weston Super Mare (pb)	1-85937-306-2	£9.99
Weymouth (pb)	1-85937-209-0	£9.99
Wiltshire (pb)	1-85937-277-5	£9.99
Wiltshire Churches (pb)	1-85937-171-x	£9.99
Wiltshire Living Memories (pb)	1-85937-396-8	£9.99
Winchester (pb)	1-85937-428-x	£9.99
Windsor (pb)	1-85937-333-x	£9.99
Wokingham & Bracknell (pb)	1-85937-329-1	£9.99
Woodbridge (pb)	1-85937-498-0	£9.99
Worcester (pb)	1-85937-165-5	£9.99
Worcestershire Living Memories	1-85937-489-1	£14.99
Worcestershire	1-85937-152-3	£14.99
York (pb)	1-85937-199-x	£9.99
Yorkshire (pb)	1-85937-186-8	£9.99
Yorkshire Coastal Memories	1-85937-506-5	£14.99
Yorkshire Dales	1-85937-502-2	£14.99
Yorkshire Living Memories (pb)	1-85937-397-6	£9.99

See Frith books on the internet at www.francisfrith.co.uk

FRITH PRODUCTS & SERVICES

Francis Frith would doubtless be pleased to know that the pioneering publishing venture he started in 1860 still continues today. Over a hundred and forty years later, The Francis Frith Collection continues in the same innovative tradition and is now one of the foremost publishers of vintage photographs in the world. Some of the current activities include:

Interior Decoration

Today Frith's photographs can be seen framed and as giant wall murals in thousands of pubs, restaurants, hotels, banks, retail stores and other public buildings throughout the country. In every case they enhance the unique local atmosphere of the places they depict and provide reminders of gentler days in an increasingly busy and frenetic world.

Product Promotions

Frith products are used by many major companies to promote the sales of their own products or to reinforce their own history and heritage. Frith promotions have been used by Hovis bread, Courage beers, Scots Porage Oats, Colman's mustard, Cadbury's foods, Mellow Birds coffee, Dunhill pipe tobacco, Guinness, and Bulmer's Cider.

Genealogy and Family History

As the interest in family history and roots grows world-wide, more and more people are turning to Frith's photographs of Great Britain for images of the towns, villages and streets where their ancestors lived; and, of course, photographs of the churches and chapels where their ancestors were christened, married and buried are an essential part of every genealogy tree and family album.

Frith Products

All Frith photographs are available Framed or just as Mounted Prints and Posters (size 23 x 16 inches). These may be ordered from the address below. From time to time other products - Address Books, Calendars, Table Mats, etc - are available.

The Internet

Already fifty thousand Frith photographs can be viewed and purchased on the internet through the Frith websites and a myriad of partner sites.

For more detailed information on Frith companies and products, look at these sites:

www.francisfrith.co.uk
www.francisfrith.com
(for North American visitors)

See the complete list of Frith Books at:

www.francisfrith.co.uk

This web site is regularly updated with the latest list of publications from the Frith Book Company. If you wish to buy books relating to another part of the country that your local bookshop does not stock, you may purchase on-line.

For further information, trade, or author enquiries please contact us at the address below:
The Francis Frith Collection, Frith's Barn, Teffont, Salisbury, Wiltshire, England SP3 5QP.
Tel: +44 (0)1722 716 376 Fax: +44 (0)1722 716 881 Email: sales@francisfrith.co.uk

See Frith books on the internet at www.francisfrith.co.uk

FREE MOUNTED PRINT

CHOOSE ANY IMAGE FROM THIS BOOK

Mounted Print
Overall size 14 x 11 inches

Fill in and cut out this voucher and return

it with your remittance for £2.25 (to cover postage and handling). Offer valid for delivery to UK addresses only.

Choose any photograph included in this book.

Your SEPIA print will be A4 in size. It will be mounted in a cream mount with a burgundy rule line (overall size 14 x 11 inches).

Order additional Mounted Prints at HALF PRICE (only £7.49 each*)

If you would like to order more Frith prints from this book, possibly as gifts for friends and family, you can buy them at half price (with no additional postage and handling costs).

Have your Mounted Prints framed

For an extra £14.95 per print* you can have your mounted print(s) framed in an elegant polished wood and gilt moulding, overall size 16 x 13 inches (no additional postage and handling required).

---

* IMPORTANT!

These special prices are only available if you order at the same time as you order your free mounted print. You must use the ORIGINAL VOUCHER on this page (no copies permitted). We can only despatch to one address.

Send completed Voucher form to:
The Francis Frith Collection, Frith's Barn, Teffont, Salisbury, Wiltshire SP3 5QP

Voucher for *FREE* and Reduced Price Frith Prints

Please do not photocopy this voucher. Only the original is valid, so please fill it in, cut it out and return it to us with your order.

Picture ref no	Page no	Qty	Mounted @ £7.49	Framed + £14.95	Total Cost
		1	Free of charge*	£	£
			£7.49	£	£
			£7.49	£	£
			£7.49	£	£
			£7.49	£	£
			£7.49	£	£
Please allow 28 days for delivery			* Post & handling (UK)		£2.25
			Total Order Cost		£

Title of this book . . . .

I enclose a cheque/postal order for £ . . . .
made payable to 'The Francis Frith Collection'

OR please debit my Mastercard / Visa / Switch / Amex card
(credit cards please on all overseas orders), details below

Card Number

Issue No (Switch only)   Valid from (Amex/Switch)

Expires   Signature

Name Mr/Mrs/Ms . . . .

Address . . . .

. . . .

. . . .

. . . . Postcode . . . .

Daytime Tel No . . . .

Email . . . .

Valid to 31/12/05

Free Print – see overleaf

Would you like to find out more about Francis Frith?

We have recently recruited some entertaining speakers who are happy to visit local groups, clubs and societies to give an illustrated talk documenting Frith's travels and photographs. If you are a member of such a group and are interested in hosting a presentation, we would love to hear from you.

Our speakers bring with them a small selection of our local town and county books, together with sample prints. They are happy to take orders. A small proportion of the order value is donated to the group who have hosted the presentation. The talks are therefore an excellent way of fundraising for small groups and societies.

Can you help us with information about any of the Frith photographs in this book?

We are gradually compiling an historical record for each of the photographs in the Frith archive. It is always fascinating to find out the names of the people shown in the pictures, as well as insights into the shops, buildings and other features depicted.

If you recognize anyone in the photographs in this book, or if you have information not already included in the author's caption, do let us know. We would love to hear from you, and will try to publish it in future books or articles.

Our production team

Frith books are produced by a small dedicated team at offices in the converted Grade II listed 18th-century barn at Teffont near Salisbury, illustrated above. Most have worked with the Frith Collection for many years. All have in common one quality: they have a passion for the Frith Collection. The team is constantly expanding, but currently includes:

Paul Baron, Jason Buck, John Buck, Ruth Butler, Heather Crisp, David Davies, Isobel Hall, Julian Hight, Peter Horne, James Kinnear, Karen Kinnear, Tina Leary, Stuart Login, David Marsh, Sue Molloy, Glenda Morgan, Wayne Morgan, Kate Rotondetto, Dean Scource, Eliza Sackett, Terence Sackett, Sandra Sampson, Adrian Sanders, Sandra Sanger, Julia Skinner, Claire Tarrier, Lewis Taylor, Shelley Tolcher, Lorraine Tuck and Jeremy Walker.